Index

It is easy and fun to dye fabrics, ribbons and lace to create dozens of beautiful projects.

With permanent markers, everyone can enjoy random coloring and the magic created when alcohol is added!

All ages love to color and create. Great projects for family night and group activities. Use only a few supplies and have a lot of fun.

So Easy - Anyone Can Do It Method
Plastic Bag Scrunching

This simple technique is fun to do and the patterns will vary depending on the way the piece was colored.

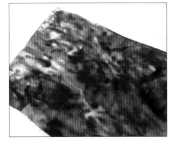

1 - Scrunching

1. Color fabric as desired.
2. Scrunch up the fabric and place it in a plastic bag.
3. Spray into the bag, close the bag, and scrunch to work the spray into the fabric.
4. Remove from bag and let it dry. Press flat.

What to Use and How to Color Fabrics

Permanent marker colors with an alcohol base will run, mix and bleed when touched with Blending Solution or alcohol. Alcohol Inks will also run, mix and bleed. Both work equally well on fabrics, lace, ribbon and thread (Silk, Cotton and Synthetic).

Protect Yourself and Your Workspace

- **Protect your clothing.** Wear old clothes or a paint shirt to protect your clothes from drips of color.
- **Protect your hands.** Wear disposable latex gloves. Clean your hands and work area with alcohol and with soap and water.
- **Protect your work surface.** Remember, these markers, inks and fluids are permanent!

Always protect your table or work surface with freezer paper (shiny side up). I use a new piece for each project.
I also cover my whole table with one large sheet of plastic for extra protection.

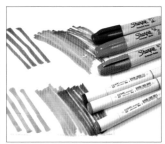   

Basic Steps for Permanent Markers

Permanent markers (Sharpie & Copic work best) come in wonderful colors and are easy to apply with chisel and brush tips. These markers with an alcohol base will bleed when touched with alcohol, but do not bleed with water.
1. Place your fabric on freezer paper (shiny side up). Color lines, shapes and marks. It is OK to blend where the colors touch.
2. Spray with Blending solution or alcohol to make the colors blend. While project is damp, mist again or add drops of alcohol. Let dry.
3. If desired, repeat coloring and misting until desired blend is reached. Let dry. Add details or more color as desired. Iron to heat-set.

Basic Steps for Alcohol Inks

Alcohol Inks have the advantage that the colors can be applied from the bottle. No marking or drawing... just drip and smudge the colors together. I often use Alcohol Inks to color large areas and to dye my background fabrics.
1. Work on freezer paper (shiny side up). Spritz the freezer paper with Blending Solution or alcohol. Drip Alcohol Inks onto the paper.
2. Splatter, blend or smudge the colors with a sponge, paintbrush, pipette dropper or stick to spread the ink as desired.
3. Place fabric on top of the wet ink and press gently to absorb the colors. To add more color, lift one edge of the fabric at a time and mist the freezer paper again. Add more drips of color. Lay the fabric down again and press gently. Let dry. Iron to heat-set.

 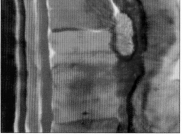 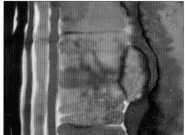

Heat-Set Colors with an Iron

Prevent further bleeding of the colors in your fabric by heat-setting the colors. Press fabric with a hot, dry iron (no steam). This helps protect colors in the fabric during washing and wearing.

How to Launder Your Fabrics

It is best to wash fabrics by hand in cold water.
The fabric on the left was washed in the washing machine on Gentle cycle in cold water with NO soap. Washing softens the color just a bit.
The fabric on the right has not been washed.

How to Color Embellishments

Have you ever spent hours looking for the perfect thread, lace, ribbon or trim to match your project only to settle for something that was almost right? Now you can quickly dye your trims to coordinate with every project.

Lace, Ribbons & Trims

You'll love coordinating everything. It is easy and quick to dye trims to coordinate with every project.
1. Color thread, ribbons, lace, flowers and trims as desired. • 2. Spray with alcohol to make the colors bleed. • 3. Let dry.

Embellishments

Perfect for any project! Color purchased florals, ribbons, buttons and dolls for fabulous one-of-a-kind table decor and centerpieces.
1. Color fabric dolls, flowers, leaves and buttons as desired. • 2. Spray with alcohol to make the colors bleed. • 3. Let dry.

Add Fun Textures

Add textures to dyed fabric with powders and oils. Use rubber stamps and found objects to texturize fabric surfaces.

Salts, Powders and Oils

Raid your kitchen pantry to find common items that will add textures, spots, and runs.

Stamps and Found Objects

Use simple canvas, mesh, sponges, combs, shapes, rubber stamps and erasers for texture.

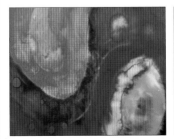 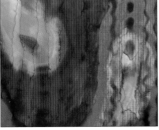 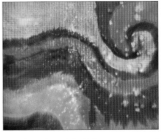 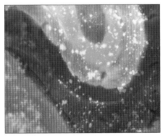

Apply liquids after the fabric is completely dry.
Left - Drops of Baby Oil
Center - Drops of Ammonia
Right - Drops of Alcohol

Apply liquids after the fabric is completely dry.
Left - Lines of Alcohol
Center - Bleach Pen (no effect)
Right - Draw with Alcohol

Apply salts while fabric is wet and let sit on fabric to dry overnight.
Left - Table Salt
Center - Sea Salt
Right - Rock Salt

Apply powders while fabric is wet, let sit on fabric to dry overnight.
Left - Corn Starch
Center - Baking Powder
Right - Baking Soda

Tie-Dye Techniques

2 - Sewing to Gather

Create a fun effect with simple sewing.
1. Using a disappearing marker, draw 6 rows of draped lines (as though you were wearing 6 necklaces). Leaving long tails, sew a Running stitch along each line. Grasping all tails together, gather the fabric tightly and tie the ends. •
2. Color the gathered area. • 3. Spray well to make the colors bleed. Let dry. Remove stitches.

3 - Folding with Binder Clips

Binder clips secure the pleats in this shirt. Because you don't color the bound areas, a pattern of white spaces is left behind.
1. Make 2 sets of 3 pleats. Secure each set with 2″ binder clips. • 2. Color each row between the clips. • 3. Spray generously to make the colors bleed. Let dry. Remove the clips.

4 - 'Under the Sea' Turtle Tee

Draw turtles and bubbles with Washable School glue for a faux-resist technique.
1. Place freezer paper (shiny side up) inside a shirt. Draw turtles and dots with washable glue. Let dry overnight. • 2. Color as desired. • 3. Spray to make the colors bleed. Let dry. Wash the glue out with water.

5 - Pleating with Rubber Bands

Here's a simple way to create a pattern of striped bands with a fabulous look.
1. Pleat a shirt and bind the pleats together with rubber bands. • 2. Color each section. •
3. Spray generously to make the colors bleed. Let dry. Remove the rubber bands.

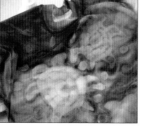

Favorite T's

Everybody wears T-shirts. Some people even collect them. Now you can design your own with simple techniques that are quick, easy and enjoyable.

Colorful design possibilities are endless, so get ready for an exciting and colorful experience.

This is a great craft to share with children. Since T-shirts are inexpensive, you can create a large number of beautiful gifts within your budget.

Audrey (age 5) and Seth (age 10) colored their own shirts with the Sunburst technique. Mom helped apply the rubber bands to be sure they were tight, then these young designers completed the shirts with markers and alcohol. What fun!

Now they want to decorate shoes and caps too.

6 – Sunburst Design

A burst of rainbow colored bands radiates from a center point on this fun shirt.

1. Place your hand inside a shirt. Pull up fabric from the center front and wrap a rubber band tightly around the tip. • 2. Shape fabric into a cone shape and secure tightly at intervals with rubber bands. • 3. Color each section. • 4. Spray generously and pour extra alcohol onto really thick sections to make the colors bleed. Let dry. Remove the rubber bands.

Delightful Dolls

Dolls and animals are truly universal, being found in every culture and every country in the world. Everywhere you go, from the most remote village to highly populated cities, you will find children of all ages enthralled with dolls.

Dolls and doll making predate recorded history and continue to thrive today. Now, you can join the time-honored tradition of making and dressing a doll of your own creation.

Dancing Doll

Delightful Dolls

Here's a great project to share with children. Doll decorating is fun and easy. Begin with a premade fabric doll.
1. Color the doll with markers or Alcohol Ink. Color extra fabric for clothing.
2. Spray to make the colors bleed. Let dry.
3. Press fabrics flat. Dress your doll.

Bunny - 4" tall
Begin with a premade furry bunny. Tie a ribbon around the neck.

Gypsy Doll - 6" tall
Begin with a premade 'Bendable' muslin doll from *FibreCraft.* Face: Color cheeks and lips with a marker. • Dress - Cut fabric 4" x 6". Gather one long side tightly at the neck. Cut slits for arm holes. Sew the back of dress closed. Place dress on doll. • Scarf - Cut fabric ¾" x 6". Tie around the neck. • Hat - Cut fabric 3" x 3". Fold into a triangle. Tie around the head.

Small Ballerina - 6" tall
Begin with a premade 'Bendable' muslin doll from *FibreCraft.* • Sew a bow to each foot. • Sew or glue curled ribbon to head for hair. • Draw lips with a marker. • Dress: Cut mini-tulle 5" x 12". Sew a Gather stitch 1" from one long side. Gather tightly around the doll's waist. Wrap waist with 4" of beaded ribbon from *EXPO International.* Tie or sew in place.

Dancing Doll - 6" tall
Begin with a premade fabric doll. • Draw eyes and mouth with a marker. Sew E beads to ankles and around the head. • Cut mini-tulle 3" x 12". Sew a Gather stitch 1" from one long side. Follow Dress directions for Small Ballerina.

Large Ballerina
SIZE: 16" tall
Begin with a premade 'Bendable' muslin doll from *FibreCraft.* • Draw mouth with a marker. Sew or glue extra ribbon and thread to head for hair. Crisscross ribbons and sew to feet and legs.• Cut 4 pieces of mini-tulle 12" x 36". Fold to 6" x 36". Sew a Gather stitch 2" from the long side. Follow Dress directions for Small Ballerina. Wrap waist with 7" of beaded ribbon from *EXPO International.*

Gossiping
SIZE: 24" x 24" canvas
Color a design with Sharpie markers then spray it with Alcohol.

Original Art – 'Painting' with Markers

Here is a new 'painting' process that I developed. It is creative and the results are always somewhat of a surprise. The colors run, bleed and mix to add a special look and texture to the Art pieces. 'Canvas' can be worked on almost anywhere and the colors are built up in beautiful layers. Add alcohol and let it dry overnight. Alter, add to and change the 'painting' along the way.

I like Copic markers for 'paintings'. Copic markers have a wonderful brush tip and are available in 100s of wonderful colors (you can also use Sharpie markers but there is a smaller color choice).

Stampede

SIZE: 24" x 24" canvas
Man's fascination with horses has been expressed from the earliest cave drawings to today's castings in bronze. Celebrate the beauty of horses with a design that is uniquely yours.
1. Draw horses.
2. Color with Copic markers as desired.
3. Spray to make the colors bleed. Let dry.
4. Add color as needed.
5. Lightly spray to make the colors bleed. Let dry.
6. Outline shapes and add color as needed.

Use a stretched canvas as the base. Stretch White Dupioni Silk or Taffeta Silk on top of the canvas, attach it to the back with staples.

1. Draw or transfer a pattern to the silk with a pencil or graphite. Go over the lines with a fine Black marker tip.
2. Use markers to add colors to areas of the design. Leave some white fabric showing as this allows the colors to flow, spread and mix when you add alcohol. I also like to leave 'strokes' showing in places as this adds interesting texture.
3. Now the fun part, spray the entire canvas with alcohol. Add a lot of alcohol to encourage runs, drips and spreading of the colors. Sometimes I tilt the canvas up about 2" in the back to encourage a few drips and runs. Lay the canvas flat and let it dry overnight
4. Use markers to brighten color areas that have faded. Also use the brush tip to strengthen some colors close to the Black outlines.
5. Spray the entire canvas with alcohol again to create more color runs and spreading. Lay the canvas flat and let it dry overnight.
6. Use a fine tip or brush tip Black marker to outline important areas of the design and to add details.

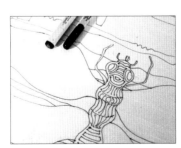

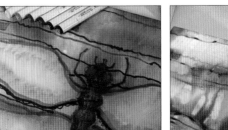

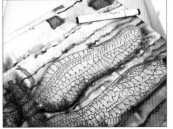

Dragonfly

SIZE: 20" x 24" canvas

As a symbol of light and joy, dragonflies are said to prompt us to unleash our creative imaginations.

1. Draw a dragonfly.
2. Color with Copic markers as desired.
3. Spray to make the colors bleed. Let dry.
4. Color again and add details.
5. Spray again to make the colors bleed. Let dry.
6. Outline shapes and draw details with a Black marker.

quilts pieced by Donna Perrotta
Tip: For these two small wall quilts we used China Silk (three 14" x 72" scarves of Habotai Silk) then ironed lightweight fusible interfacing on the back to give the fabric body.

Color Wheel Quilt

quilted by Susan Corbett - SIZE: 23" x 23"
1. Create your own rainbow fabric by drawing lines of color. Lay fabric flat, then spray with alcohol to make the colors bleed. Let dry.

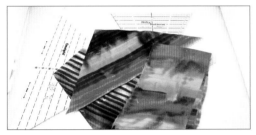

2. Cut 1 scarf into 8 triangles with a *Nifty Notions* 45° Kaleidoscope ruler. Also cut 4 corner triangles with *Omnigrid* #98 Diagonal Triangle ruler. Sew the triangles in a wheel shape. • 3. Cut a 1" x 61" strip for the inner border. Sew in place. Cut the other scarf into $4^{1}/4"$ strips. Sew as a border. 4. Layer, quilt and bind the edges.

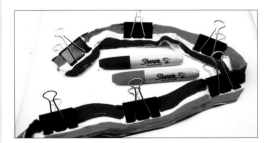

Tie-Dye Strips Quilt

quilted by Susan Corbett - SIZE:19" x 24"
1. Fold, clip and mark on fabric, see page 32. Lay fabric flat, then spray with alcohol. Let dry.

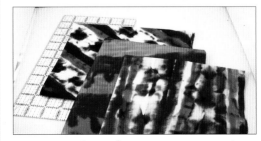

2. Cut 1 scarf into $1^{1}/2"$ strips. Cut a second scarf into $2^{1}/2"$ strips. Sew the strips together. 3. Cut the third scarf into $3^{1}/2"$ strips. Sew in place as a border.
4. Layer, quilt, and bind the edges.

Color your own beautiful fabric with markers. For this original quilt I created a center panel with large 'square' motifs, Draw squares with markers. Lay flat then spray with alcohol to bleed the colors. Let dry.

'Color Blocks' Art Quilt

quilted by Sue Needle
SIZE: 29" x 41"

Color a center panel, then add pieced fabric borders and little banners to hang at the bottom. Fabric: 3 yards of Dupioni Silk (or Taffeta Silk). These wonderful fabrics are lightweight and have body, making them easy to sew.

Center Panel - Create a center panel with large 'square' motifs. Applique bits of fabric in the center of each block for texture. Embellish as desired.

Top Border - Piece 3 strips 1$^1/2$" wide to make a border. Sew the border to the quilt.

Right Border - Sew 2 strips 2$^1/2$" x length of quilt in place. Cut 21 squares 2$^1/2$" and fold into triangles. Position along the edge and sew in place.

Left Border - Make 10 Hourglass blocks 4" x 4". Sew together as a border. Sew in place.

Bottom Border - Randomly sew 1$^1/2$" squares together to make 4 strips 1$^1/2$" wide. Sew the strips together as a border. Sew to the bottom of the quilt.

Flags - Cut 12 squares 5$^1/2$" x 5$^1/2$". Match up 6 pairs. Cut into a flag shape. Sew the raw edges leaving the 5$^1/2$" side open for turning. Turn right side out. Press. Sew to the bottom of the quilt after quilting but before binding.

Finishing - Layer with batting and backing, quilt as desired and bind the edges.

Small Art Quilts

In the last thirty years, quilts have leaped the chasm from traditional folk crafts to museums and galleries as significant as the Smithsonian Institute and the New York Metropolitan Museum of Art.

Art quilts continue to redefine our concept of quilting and breathe new life into old traditions. Don't miss this opportunity to join those who love fiber and hand-dyed fabrics as a means of personal expression. Expand your artistic possibilities with vibrant, creative energy.

Day in a Garden Applique Shirt

I want one of those!

Prepare yourself to hear this often when you wear your new favorite shirt. This simple applique technique is beautiful. Nearly every machine has a Zig-zag stitch, so enjoy a fun afternoon designing a unique shirt that everyone will love.

Unleash your imagination and have fun.

Create colorful fabrics for leaves and flowers. 1. Draw colors on fabric (we used China Silk two 14" x 72" Habotai Silk scarves, Taffeta Silk also works well). Lay fabric flat, then spray with alcohol to make the colors bleed. Let dry. Iron Steam-A-Seam 2 to the back of the dyed fabric. • 2. Draw grass lines on the shirt with a disappearing marker. Position tear-away stabilizer behind the design. • 3. Loosely Zig-zag stitch grass lines with Green thread. • 4. Cut out assorted stems and leaves from Green dyed fabric. Position stems and leaves randomly on the shirt, then iron in place. Zig-zag stitch in place with Green thread. • 5. Cut out circles for flowers and centers from Red/Blue dyed fabric. Position flowers on the shirt, then iron in place. Glue any loose edges. • 6. Zig-zag stitch around the flower centers and outer circles with Red thread. Add additional stitches as desired. Pull extra thread to the back and secure with a knot. Remove stabilizer. Remember to wash your shirt by hand. Refer to pattern guides on pages 48 - 49.

Luxury Scarves

Create sumptuous scarves to match your every mood!

Experiment with different silk fabrics for exquisite results. The scarves on the left and right are made from Habotai Silk; the two center scarves are lush Silk Velvet.

SIZE: 14" x 72" scarves

Left Scarf - 'Do the Twist' Sunbursts of Color on China Silk, see page 25 for design tips

Center Left Scarf - Rainbows of Color on Silk Velvet with Lines, see page 20 for design tips

Center Right Scarf - Squares of Color on Silk Velvet, see page 13 for design tips for 'squares'

Right Scarf - Fold and Clip Lines of Color on China Silk, see page 32 for design tips.

Basic Instructions for 'Stitched Collage'

Whether you want a single flower, a whole garden, a pretty face, or creative motifs, the 'Stitched Collage' technique will thrill everyone who appreciates the beauty of varied stitches, hand-dyed fabrics, quilted layers and delightful creations.

Refer to these basic steps as a guide to your personal Art Quilt.

'Round and Round' Flower SIZE: 9" x 14"

I chose this fabric collage flower for the basic instructions. It includes all of the basics for fabric preparation, stitching, quilting and binding plus extra creative tips for ruching, gathering and bead embellishment. Use these basic instructions to create your own art piece and for reference on how to make the additional pieces on pages 18 - 34.

Dye assorted colors on fabrics with Permanent Markers or Alcohol Inks (refer to pages 2, 4 and 5).

Applique - I used China Silk (a 14" x 72" scarf of Habotai Silk). You can also use assorted fabrics such as cheesecloth, lace, organza, Taffeta Silk, Dupioni Silk, mesh, ribbon and assorted scraps for the applique pieces.

Background - I used Dupioni Silk. Bleached muslin, lightweight White canvas and Taffeta Silk also work well.

Lay fabrics flat, then spray with alcohol to make the colors bleed. Let dry.

Iron Steam-A-Seam 2 to the back of all the dyed fabrics.

1. Gather all the materials, dyed fabrics, threads, etc. • 2. Position and adhere tear-away stabilizer behind the background fabric. Draw placement outlines of designs with a disappearing marker. Cut out assorted shapes from applique fabrics. Position applique shapes randomly on the background then iron in place. Glue any loose edges with a washable glue stick. • 3. Zig-zag stitch in place with matching thread. • 4. Check on the back of the piece to be sure that all stitches are secure.

   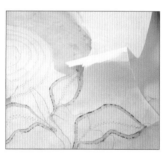

5. Sew a long tube of dyed fabric and turn it right side out. Gather stitch down the center of the tube. Gather it up to form a ruched edge. Iron the flower center in place above the stem. Sew ruching down the center of the tube so it fits around the center circle. • 6. Tear a long strip of dyed fabric. Fold the strip in half. Wrap the folded strip around the center. Sew the strip in place, working each row around the center. • 7. Leave a small space between the rows and use a pointed stick to slightly gather and coax the strip in place as you sew. Pull the thread tails to the back and tie off. • 8. Tear away the stabilizer off of the back when all applique is completed.

9. Layer the decorated piece, quilt batting and backing. • 10. Quilt the background with free-motion quilting (refer to page 39). • 11. Sew beads around the flower (page 35). • 12. Bind the edges as desired. Cut a 2¼" strip of fabric and fold it in half. Match the edges and sew binding around the edges (miter the corners). Turn binding to the back and stitch in place.

Refer to page 43
for pattern guide

SIZE: 2¹/₂" x 3¹/₂"
Layer pieces and applique as desired. Add hand-embroidered stitches and embellishments to personalize your ATC.
Layer with quilt batting and backing. Bind the edges with fabric or Zigzag stitches.
Refer to page 42.

ATC's - Artist Trading Cards

Decorate little works of art with dyed fabrics. As art that fits in your pocket or wallet, Artist Trading Cards are wonderful ways to share your creativity with others. Made in the size of traditional baseball cards, these little projects are both inexpensive and fun to make.

Creative Patterns for Markers

7 - Angled Lines

Create movement by drawing irregular lines. The color changes create the illusion of curves as well as patches of light and dark resulting in a wonderful texture.
1. Draw lines as shown.
2. Spray to make the colors bleed. Let dry.

8 - Stormy Sunset

Dark Blue and Orange combine in a powerful clash of lines that result in a tantalizing display. A bold hand scoured the color on quickly. This is an easy technique that is fun to do.
1. Scribble the lines as shown.
2. Spray to make the colors bleed. Let dry.

Postcards

Surprise someone you love at the mailbox. Nothing says "I'm thinking of you" and makes someone feel special like a hand-crafted card.

Cheer up a friend, celebrate a birthday, or send a note "just because" with a one-of-a-kind card. Slip it into a clear envelope and send it through the mail today.

Bluebirds

SIZE: 5" x 7"

Stamp the background with a swirl and StazOn ink before adding applique designs. Layer pieces and applique as desired. Add Straight stitches for the beaks. Add small beads for eyes.

Friends

SIZE: 4" x 6"

Layer pieces and applique as desired. Add purchased printed ribbon for the words and dye it.

Layer with quilt batting and backing. Bind the edges with fabric or Rickrack. Refer to page 50 for patterns..

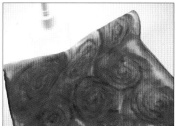

9 - Going in Circles

Whether your creativity is spinning out of control or you just like to express its infinite possibilities, you will enjoy the ease and simplicity of this flowing design.
1. Fill the material with large spirals.
2. Spray to make the colors bleed. Let dry.

10 - Fenced In

As you can see in this project, you don't have to draw a large number of lines to get a lot of color. Primary colors are always a good place to begin when trying out combinations.
1. Draw 6-8 lines per box, alternating colors.
2. Spray to make the colors bleed. Let dry.

Back of Purse

Carry-All Purse

Keep your wallet, a few dollars and a few essentials safely at hand in an attractive purse designed with applique, collage and quilting.

Add free motion quilting in the background to add texture and sturdy durability.

SIZE: 6" x 10"

Cut a backing fabric 10" x 13". Layer pieces and applique as desired. Cut scraps of organza for backing behind the small hearts. Add scraps of organza for backing behind the small hearts. The word "journey" is a piece of printed ribbon. Add Rickrack and bead embellishments to your purse (page 37).

Layer the finished piece with quilt batting and backing. Bind the top edge with fabric. Quilt the background. Fold the background piece in half with right sides together. Stitch the side seam. Insert beaded fringe into the bottom seam and stitch. Turn purse right side out. Sew on cording for the handle.

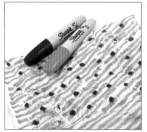
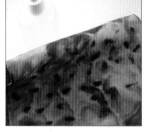

Creative Patterns for Markers

11 - Parallel Lines

Stripes are one of the easiest designs to make and they never go out of style. The design will be most prominent if you choose colors with a high contrast, such as red and blue. Colors such as orange and yellow or pink and apricot will create a softer blend.
1. Color as desired.
2. Spray to make the colors bleed. Let dry. Press flat.

12 - Lines & Dots

Thin lines only bleed a little, leaving a softer color than dark dots. The combination possibilities with this technique are endless, so use your imagination and don't be afraid to experiment with variations in color, line thickness and dot size.
1. Draw lines and dots as desired.
2. Spray to make the colors bleed. Let dry. Press flat.

Refer to pattern guide
on page 45.

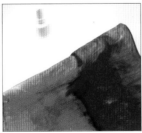

13 - Thick & Thin Lines

Some lines are thicker than others, creating a rich, deep color. Changing the width of the spaces between the lines will alter the bleed, making each project unique.
1. Draw lines as desired.
2. Spray to make the colors bleed. Let dry. Press flat.

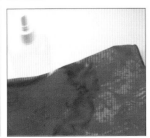

14 - Lighter Shades

Using colors in a similar shade, like Pink and Red will result in a very attractive subtle and soft bleed. In this sample, the colors change near the middle of the piece.
1. Draw lines as desired.
2. Spray to make the colors bleed. Let dry. Press flat.

Rubber Stamping

15 - Embossing Powder

Embossing with an ink pad and powder forms a resist pattern on fabric.
1. Stamp the design, sprinkle embossing powder. Emboss with a heat gun. • 2. Color as desired. • 3. Spray to make the colors bleed. Let dry. Press flat.

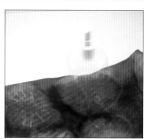

16 - Embossing Ink

Embossing ink will make light designs on fabric. Create areas that resist Permanent markers and Alcohol Inks.
1. Use an embossing ink pad to stamp a design on fabric. Let it dry. • 2. Color as desired. • 3. Spray to make the colors bleed. Let dry. Press flat.

Stitched Hangings

Create a stitched collage memento that will be treasured. Copy family photos and vintage postcards onto computer fabric to add to the collage.

Family Memories Hanging

by Barbara Burnett

When I look at this photo of my grandparents as newlyweds, I can't help wondering about their hopes and dreams for the future. I doubt they ever imagined that someday they would have grandchildren who so adored them. Thankful for so many cherished memories, my brother and I often reminisce about our carefree summers spent with Grandpa and Grandma on their Iowa farm.

SIZE: 11" x 14"

You'll need: Computer fabric sheets from *Jacquard* to make fabric prints from your photos
• Dyed fabric for the background 13" x 13"
• Dyed fabric scraps, lace and netting for applique
• Dyed embellishments (rose, Pearl Cotton floss, buttons, ribbon) • Brocade fabric • *Stampabilities* Rubber stamp and ink pad • Quilt batting • Dowel rod • Embellishments • Braid fringe and tassels.

1. Rubber stamp design on a corner of 12" x 13" dyed fabric. Let dry. • 2. Print vintage wedding photo and marriage license on computer fabric. Remove backing and trim leaving a fabric border. Fray the edges. • 3. Layer fabrics and photo on background. Stitch around appliques and photo. • 4. Layer the finished piece with quilt batting and backing. Quilt the background. • 5. Add ribbon, wedding rings, embellishments, rose netting, lace and buttons. • 6. Create a tube with brocade fabric. Stitch a tube to the top and stitch trim across the bottom edge. • 7. Insert a dowel rod through fabric tube. Tie tassels to the rod and hang.

Country Home

Placid and welcoming, the pastel background captures the serenity of a sunrise or sunset, reassuring us once more that there's no place like home.

SIZE: 10" x 12"

Layer pieces and applique as desired (refer to page 16).
Layer with quilt batting and backing. Bind the edges with fabric.
Refer to page 40 for pattern guide.

17 - Permanent Ink

Stamp and color - it's not just for paper anymore! Use your favorite rubber stamp with StazOn ink.
1. Stamp design on fabric with StazOn ink. Let dry. • 2. Color with markers or Alcohol inks as desired. • 3. Spray to make the colors bleed. Let dry. Press flat.

18 - Texture Plate

Textures create wonderful back designs. Use part of a rubber placemat or plastic canvas as a stamp.
1. Rub StazOn ink over the surface of the texture. Press texture onto fabric. Let dry.
2. Color with markers as desired.
3. Spray to make the colors bleed. Let dry.

Rubber Band Ties

19 - Wrapped Pen

Create splashes of dyed color by wrapping an old pen with a plastic barrel.
1. Wrap pen, secure with rubber bands.
• 2. Color with markers. • 3. Spray to make the colors bleed. Allow to dry. •
4. Remove rubber bands. Press flat.

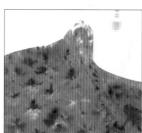

20 - Wrapped Ruler

For striking parallel stripes, try this simple technique.
1. Wrap a plastic ruler, keeping the material flat. Secure with rubber bands.
• 2. Color with markers. • 3. Spray to make the colors bleed. Allow to dry. •
4. Remove rubber bands. Press flat.

Hangings

Make a collage hanging with scraps of hand-dyed fabrics. Small beads and embellishments add to the collage.

Tropical Flower

Brighten your day with a tropical flower set against the refreshingly cool colors of a rain forest. This gorgeous flower is fun to layer and easy to make.

SIZE: 7" x 10"

Layer pieces. Position a piece of organza behind the flower. Add premade satin leaves from a bridal store.

Applique as desired (refer to page 16).

Sew beads around the flower center (page 35).

Layer with quilt batting and backing. Bind the edges with fabric.

Refer to pattern guide on page 44.

This Way
by Paula Pillow

Depict modern life in high gear. An arrow points the way in this eclectic work of art.

SIZE: 10" x 12"

Layer pieces and applique as desired (refer to page 16). Layer with quilt batting and backing. Add decorative threads to add dimension - couch around the arrow, add knots in the corner. Layer with batting. Bind the outside by stitching over the raw fabric edges.

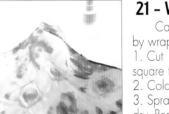
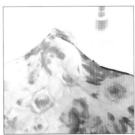

21 – Wrapped Chipboard Squares

Capture the effect of old block printing by wrapping squares.
1. Cut 1" chipboard squares. Wrap each square tightly and secure with rubber bands.
2. Color fabric and squares with markers.
3. Spray to make the colors bleed. Allow to dry. Remove the rubber bands. Press flat.

22 – 'Do the Twist' Sunburst

Try a twist for unexpected bursts of pattern and radiant color.
1. Fold fabric in quarters. Begin twisting at the folded point and secure tightly with rubber bands. • 2. Color with markers. • 3. Spray to make the colors bleed. Allow to dry. • 4. Remove the rubber bands. Press flat.

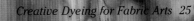

Colors of Sharpie Markers

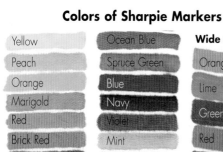

		Wide Chisel Tip
Yellow	Ocean Blue	Orange
Peach	Spruce Green	Lime
Orange	Blue	Green
Marigold	Navy	Red
Red	Violet	Purple
Brick Red	Mint	Turquoise
Berry	Lime	Blue
Magenta	Olive	Black
Pink	Green	
Boysenberry	Brown	
Purple	Burgundy	
Lilac	Black	

Copic Markers & Refill Inks

Y17 Golden Yellow	Y17 Amethyst	G09 Veronese Green
Y15 Cad. Yellow	BY08 Blue Violet	G17 Forest Green
Y26 Mustard	B12 Ice Blue	G28 Ocean Green
YR04 Chrome Orange	B32 Pale Blue	R02 Flesh
YR68 Orange	B34 Manganese	E04 Lipstick Natural
YR09 Chinese Orange	B63 Light Hydrangea	E37 Sepia
R24 Prawn	BG15 Aqua	E09 Burnt Sienna
R29 Lipstick Red	BG73 Ice Cream	E29 Burnt Umber
RV29 Crimson	B24 Sky	B678 Bronze
R39 Garnet	B29 Ultramarine	BV29 Slate
RV06 Cerise	B39 Prussian Blue	Black
RV14 Begonia Pink	BG93 Green Gray	
RZZ Light Prawn	YG03 Yellow Green	
RV17 Deep Magenta	G24 Willow	
	YG06 Yellowish Green	
V04 Lilac	G02 Spectrum Green	
V15 Mallow	BG13 Mint Green	
	YG09 Lettuce Green	
	G07 Nile Green	

Colors of Alcohol Inks

Cranberry	Stream	Currant
Watermelon	Pool	Rust
Shell Pink	Aqua	Caramel
Red Pepper	Denim	Meadow
Mountain Rose	Sailboat Blue	Oregano
Salmon	Cloudy Blue	Pesto
Terra Cotta	Purple Twilight	Stonewash
Sunset Orange	Cool Pen	Raisin
Peach Bellini	Wild Plum	Latte
Butterscotch	Raspberry	Ginger
Sunshine Yellow	Pink Sherbet	Slate
Lemonade	Eggplant	Pitch
Lettuce	Espresso	
Citrus	Hazelnut	
Willow	Sandal	
Bottle	Mushroom	
Clover	Pebble	
Juniper	Lake Mist	

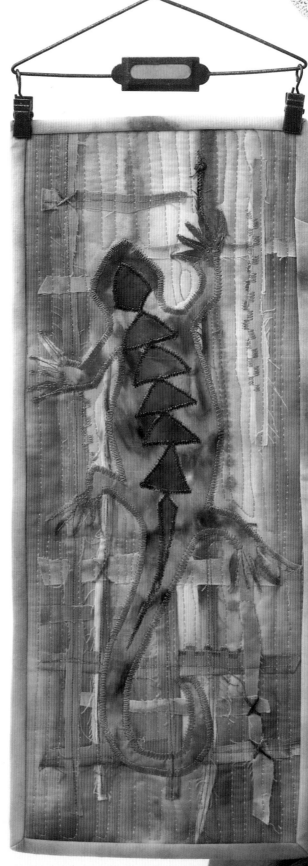

Friendly Gecko

Add a bit of colorful Southwestern desert to your decor with this charming wall hanging. Native to warm climates all over the world, geckos eat insect pests. These friendly critters are the only member of the lizard family that chirps.

SIZE: 6" x 14"

Layer pieces. Loosely weave torn strips on the background and iron in place. Add the gecko over weaving. Applique as desired (refer to page 16).

Layer with quilt batting and backing. Bind the edges with fabric.

Refer to page 42 for pattern guide.

Stitched and Wrapped 'Shibori' Techniques

'Shibori' is a Japanese term for the process of dyeing cloth in patterns using techniques that include binding, stitching, folding, twisting, and scrunching or compressing the fabric to form a resist pattern when it is dyed.

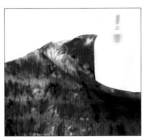

23 - Kumo Shibori

Kumo Shibori involves pleated and bound resist. Binding at regular intervals results in a regular pattern
1. Pleat a length of fabric and tie tightly with thread at regular intervals to create puffs. • 2. Color with markers. • 3. Spray to make the colors bleed. Let dry. Remove the thread ties. Press flat.

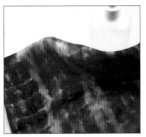

24 - Nui Shibori

Nui Shibori uses stitching to gather and compress the fabric. Tight gathers produce greater variance in color intensity.
1. Fold fabric and sew a Running stitch down the middle. Gather tightly and knot securely. • 2. Color as shown. • 3. Spray to make the colors bleed. Let dry. Remove Running stitches and press flat.

25 - Arashi Shibori

This Shibori creates diagonal patterns suggesting lines of driving rain from a storm.
1. Fold, twist and wrap material tightly around a post such as a thread spool or thick dowel. • 2. Color as shown. Unwrap and move the spool down. Wrap and color again. Repeat. • 3. Spray to make the colors bleed. Let dry. Press flat.

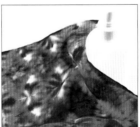

26 - Shibori Combo

This example is both pleated and stitched.
1. Fold pleats and sew a Running stitch across the top of the piece. • 2. Color in three different bands. • 3. Spray to make the colors bleed. Let dry. Remove stitches. Press flat.

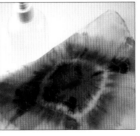

27 - Shibori Twist

Shibori is a process of dyeing cloth in patterns using wrapping and binding techniques to form a resist for fabric.
1. Tightly twist fabric into a cone shape. Tie securely by twisting thread around the cone. • 2. Color in bands to produce a starburst effect. 3. Spray to make the colors bleed. Let dry. Untie and press flat.

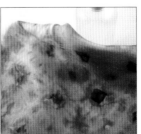

28 - Chipboard Triangles

Create fun shapes with triangles. Use rubber bands to tie this version of Shibori.
1. Cut 1" squares on the diagonal. • 2. Wrap and secure each triangle tightly with rubber bands. • 3. Color with markers. Spray to make the colors bleed. Let dry. Remove the rubber bands. Press flat.

Doodle on Fabric with Stickles & Scribbles

  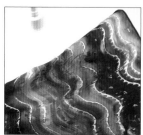

29 – Wiggles

Stickles and Scribbles provide a vibrant, permanent sheen, giving your project extra sparkle.
1. Apply Scribbles Iridescent to fabric. While wet, drag a comb over the liquid to form little lines. Let dry overnight. •
2. Color with markers. • 3. Spray to make the colors bleed. Let dry. Press flat.

  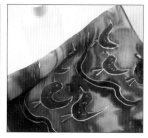

30 – Birds and Waves

Give your background the look of professional embossing with this easy technique.
1. Draw a simple design as you apply Scribbles White to fabric. Let dry overnight. • 2. Color with markers. •
3. Spray to make the colors bleed. Let dry. Press flat.

  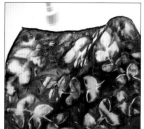

31 – Leaf Stamp

Create attractive patterns with solid design foam stamps. The design shows through the color beautifully.
1. Using a sponge, apply Scribbles White to a foam stamp. Stamp fabric. Let dry overnight. • 2. Color around the stamped areas with markers. • 3. Spray to make the colors bleed. Let dry. Press flat.

32 – Texture Plate

Textures create an interesting look. Choose plates with bold textures. The results can be beautifully subtle.
1. Using a sponge, apply Scribbles White onto texture plate. Press the plate onto fabric. Let dry overnight. • 2. Color with markers. • 3. Spray to make the colors bleed. Let dry. Press flat.

33 – Rubber Stamp

Choose a stamp with open areas and solid areas to create pockets of intense color and spaces of soft contrast.
1. Using a sponge, apply Scribbles White to a rubber stamp. Stamp fabric. Let dry overnight. • 2. Color over the stamped areas with markers. • 3. Spray to make the colors bleed. Let dry. Press flat.

34 – Wood Grain Tool

For new texture ideas, check out the paint department of your local hardware store for a wide assortment of texture tools.
1. Using a sponge, apply Scribbles White to a texture tool. Stamp onto fabric. Let dry overnight. • 2. Color with markers. •
3. Spray to make the colors bleed. Let dry. Press flat.

Elegant Lady

Delicate and demure, this beautiful woman could be a replica of goddess or a young lady contemplating her recent marriage proposal. In any case, like Mona Lisa, she seems to be keeping her secrets to herself.

SIZE: 10" x 12"

Use markers to color fabric Orange and color 2 Red round circles for cheeks. Let dry. Draw the face pattern on fabric with a disappearing marker. Machine Zig-zag stitch the facial features by varying the stitch width. Position face and neck on the background fabric.

Layer pieces and applique as desired (refer to page 16). Use ribbon printed with 'Follow Your Dreams'.

Layer with quilt batting and backing. Bind the edges with fabric.

Refer to pattern guide on pages 46 - 47.

Birds Singing at Sunrise

The trees have already dropped their leaves on this bright day, but it's so sunny that the birds have not yet flown south. You'll enjoy the rich color possibilities when you dye your own fabrics.

SIZE: 11" x 13"

Layer pieces and applique as desired (refer to page 16). Slightly gather the wings to add dimension. Embellish with ribbon flowers.

Layer with quilt batting and backing. Bind the edges with fabric.

Refer to page 41 for pattern guide.

Washable School Glue for Resists – Gel and Clear

35 – Swimming Fish
Washable Gel glue acts as a resist, saving the fabric area where it is applied.
1. Draw fish and waves with gel glue. Let dry overnight. • 2. Color the shapes roughly with markers. • 3. Spray to make the colors bleed. Let dry. Heat set with an iron. Wash with water to remove the glue.

  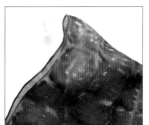

36 – Windowpanes
Use rubber stamps and washable gel glue to create exciting, new designs.
1. Apply glue to a rubber stamp with a sponge. Stamp fabric. Let dry overnight. • 2. Color with markers. • 3. Spray to make the colors bleed. Let dry. Heat set with an iron. Wash with water to remove the glue.

  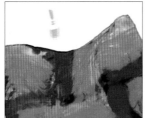

37 – Stair Steps
Foam stamps and washable clear glue will also create resist patterns.
1. Apply glue to a foam stamp with a sponge. Stamp fabric. Let dry overnight. • 2. Color with markers. • 3. Spray to make the colors bleed. Let dry. Heat set with an iron. Wash with water to remove the glue.

38 – Swirly Waves
Soft and subtle patterns emerge through colors with this resist technique.
1. Apply glue to a rubber stamp with a sponge. Stamp fabric. Let dry overnight. • 2. Color with markers. • 3. Spray to make the colors bleed. Let dry. Heat set with an iron. Wash with water to remove the glue.

39 – Geometric
Squares provide color samples.
1. Apply clear washable glue to a rubber stamp with a sponge. Stamp fabric. Let dry overnight. • 2. Color with markers. • 3. Spray to make the colors bleed. Let dry. Heat set with an iron. Wash with water to remove the glue.

40 – Triangles
Color in any pattern or design.
1. Apply clear washable glue to a rubber stamp with a sponge. Stamp fabric. Let dry overnight. • 2. Color with markers. • 3. Spray to make the colors bleed. Let dry. Heat set with an iron. Wash with water to remove the glue.

  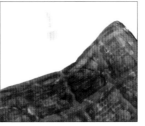

41 – Squares
Color a pattern over your design.
1. Apply clear washable glue to a rubber stamp with a sponge. Stamp fabric. Let dry overnight. • 2. Color with markers. • 3. Spray to make the colors bleed. Let dry. Heat set with an iron. Wash with water to remove the glue.

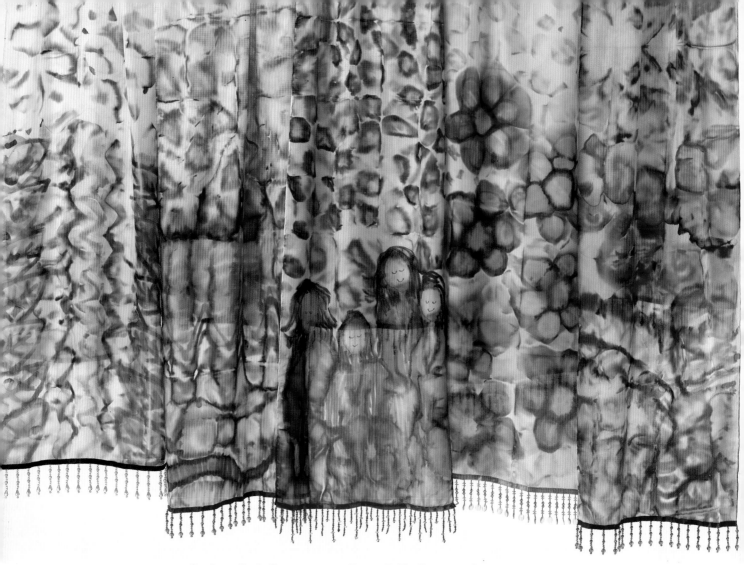

Colorful Scarves for All Occasions

*More striking than jewelry, attractive silk scarves - in China Silk or Velvet Silk -
make an enduring fashion statement. Whether your mood is playful and carefree*

Clips, Clamps and Chipboard

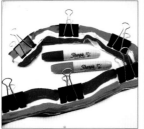

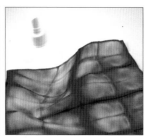

42 - Fold and Clip

Create beautiful lines of color.
1. Make 6 accordion folds along the length of a fabric scarf. Press the folds. Apply 2" binder clips along one edge of the fold. • 2. Apply color with markers. • 3. Spray well and allow the colors to bleed. Let dry. Remove the clips. Press flat.

43 - Clip Chipboard Squares

Create fabulous subtle shading.
1. Pleat fabric 4 times along the length of a fabric scarf. Use an iron to press the folds. Clamp two 2" chipboard squares over the end. • 2. Apply color with markers. • 3. Spray well and allow the color to bleed. Let dry. Remove the clips. Press flat.

or formal and refined, you can design a scarf that fits your wardrobe beautifully. Adding purchased beaded fringe gives your scarf a gorgeous professional finish for a look that is simply dazzling.

You'll love the fun techniques in this book. The more you experiment with colors, the more successful combinations you'll have.

44 – Clip a Series of Squares

Add strong colors in one easy step.
1. Fold a fabric scarf in half and pleat each end. • 2. Clamp six 2" chipboard squares along the pleated edge. •
3. Apply colors with markers. • 4. Spray generously and allow the colors to bleed. Let dry. Remove the clips. Press flat.

45 – Clip Triangles

The color secrets lie in the folding!
1. Cut a 2½" chipboard square on the diagonal to make 2 triangles. • 2. Fold fabric in half. Pleat one end. • 3. Fold the pleated ends to meet in the middle forming an arrow shape. • 4. Clamp chipboard over the pleated arrow. • 5. Color with markers. Let dry. Remove clips. Press flat.

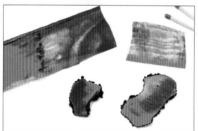

Singed Rose Petals

by Paula Pillow

Singed edges create a fabulous effect, giving rose petals and other shapes both reality and intriguing texture.

Use simple shapes and open spaces to create elegant collage art that is a joy to view.

Note: Only use China Silk for singing because it usually only singes but does not catch on fire.

SIZE: 12" x 15"

Layer pieces and applique as desired (refer to page 16). Embellish with metallic thread, sparkle yarn, and embroidery stitches. Layer with quilt batting and backing. Leave the edges unfinished for a shabby look.

46 - Burning the Edges of China Silk

Working over a bowl of water, use a wooden kitchen match to singe the edges of 'China Silk'. If the silk burns too much, simply drop it in the bowl of water to put out the fire. You'll love this process and the singed edges create a great texture and subtle shading.

Note: Do not let children play with matches or singe any fabric.

Creative Ideas for the Edges of Applique

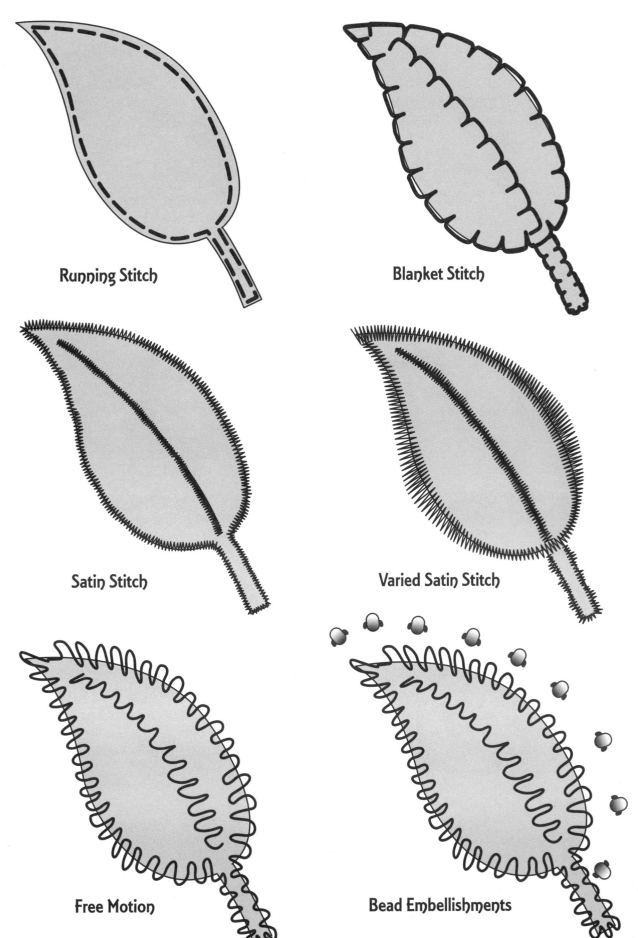

Running Stitch

Blanket Stitch

Satin Stitch

Varied Satin Stitch

Free Motion

Bead Embellishments

Embroidery Stitches

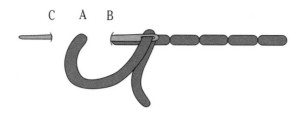

Backstitch

Come up at A, go in at B, come up again at C. Repeat, going back into same hole at A as the last stitch. Keep stitches uniform in size.

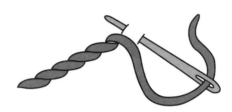

Stem Stitch

Work from left to right to make regular, slanting stitches along the stitch line. Bring the needle up above the center of the last stitch. Also called "Outline" stitch.

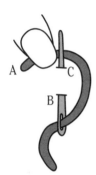

Blanket Stitch

Come up at A, hold the thread down with your thumb, go down at B. Come back up at C with the needle tip over the thread. Pull the stitch into place. Repeat, outlining with the bottom legs of the stitch. Use this stitch to edge fabrics.

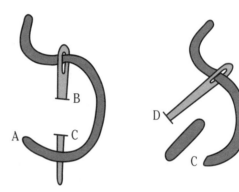

Cross Stitch

Make a diagonal Straight stitch (up at A, down at B) from lower left to upper right. Come up at C and go down at D to make another diagonal Straight stitch the same length as the first one. The stitch will form an X.

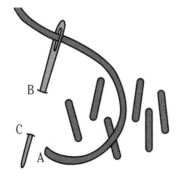

Seed Stitch

Bring needle to front of fabric (A). Insert back into fabric (B). Bring out at beginning of next stitch (C). This stitch can be used to fill in areas. The stitches should be placed irregularly and without making patterns.

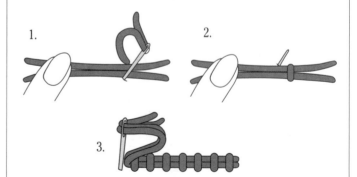

Couching Stitch

1. With your thumb, hold down one or more threads. With another thread, come up at A, go in at B. 2. Come up at C and in at D, tacking down horizontal threads. 3. When finished with a row of couching, put ends of horizontal thread in needle and pull through to back side of fabric.

and Creative Hand Stitching Ideas

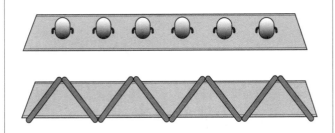

Bead Embellished Couching Over Ribbon

Sew round beads along the center of the ribbon with a Running stitch. Sew bugle beads over a ribbon, catching the edge of the ribbon with each stitch. Begin with the needle under the ribbon. Come up through ribbon edge, into bead, down into ribbon edge. Repeat until ribbon is covered.

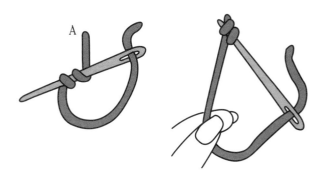

French Knot

Come up at A. Wrap the floss around the needle 2 - 3 times. Insert the needle close to A. Hold the floss and pull the needle through the loops gently.

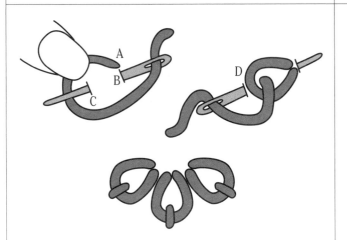

Lazy Daisy Stitch

Come up at A. Go down at B (right next to A) to form a loop. Come back up at C with the needle tip over the thread. Go down at D to make a small anchor stitch over the top of the loop.

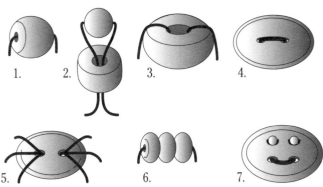

Stitching with Beads & Buttons

1. Stitch a single bead. 2. Thread a bead on top of a bead. 3. Sew each side of a bead with a single stitch. 4. Sew a single stitch across the button. 5. Sew 3 single stitches from each hole to the outside of the button. 6. Sew a group of beads together. 7. Sew a bead in two holes of a button and a single stitch through the other 2 holes.

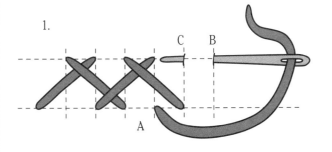
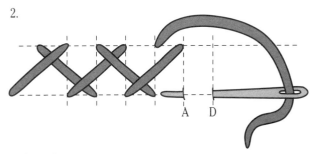

Herringbone Stitch

1. Come up at A. Make a slanted stitch to the top right, inserting the needle at B. Come up a short distance away at C.
2. Insert the needle at D to complete the stitch. Bring the needle back up at the next A to begin a new stitch. Repeat.

Machine Stitches

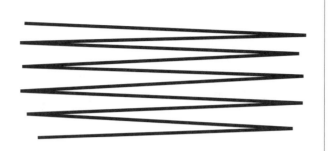

Straight Stitch

Set your machine for Straight stitches. Raise the feed dogs. Sew lines in a back and forth manner. Decorative threads look lovely here.

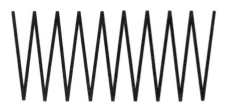

Zig-zag Stitch

Zig-zag stitches will secure an applique in place, hold a hem, or just add a decorative feature. Be sure to experiment with different stitch lengths and widths.

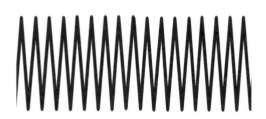

Satin Stitch

Create a smooth surface that looks solid. Practice turning corners and maneuvering curves before using this one on your final project.

Blanket Stitch

This traditional stitch was originally used to hem blankets. Today, this decorative stitch is used for applique and embellishing designs. Experiment with altering the stitch length.

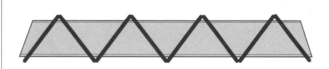

Couching Stitch

Perfect for attaching those gorgeous decorative threads that can't be run through your machine and attaching everything from ribbon to rat-tail. Simply Zig-zag stitch over your ribbon, cord, or thread.

Dense Stitching

Create a support backing for dense embroidery patterns by stitching back and forth across an area. When this is done with metallic threads, the stitching itself becomes a fabulous embellishment.

and Creative Machine Stitching Ideas

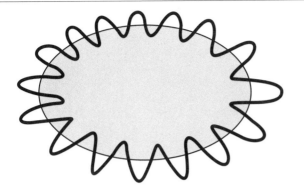

Free Motion Straight Stitch

We recommend using a Spring needle for free motion work. Be sure to lower the feed dogs. You may prefer to hoop the fabric. Move the fabric smoothly in a continuous motion around the shape.

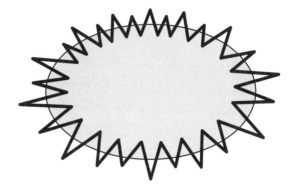

Free Motion Zig-Zag Stitch

Using a Spring needle, drop the feed dogs and set the machine on a Zig-Zag stitch. You must move the fabric when performing free motion work.

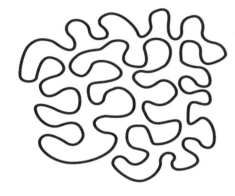

Free Motion Stippling

Stippling is a wandering stitch in which the lines do not cross.

Free Motion Swirl Stitching

Use this stitch to fill in empty areas. Begin at a point and spiral out until the space is full.

Free Motion Decorative Quilting Stitches

This process is much like doodling with your sewing machine. The most important word in the title is Free. Feel free to create whatever design inspires you.

Country Home

see page 23

Use this pattern as a guide to create your own collage.

Birds Singing at Sunrise
see page 30

Use this pattern as a guide to create your own collage.
Enlarge the pattern to 120%.

ATCs
see page 18
Use these patterns as a guide to
create your own collage.

Friendly Gecko
see page 26
Use this pattern as a guide to create your own collage.

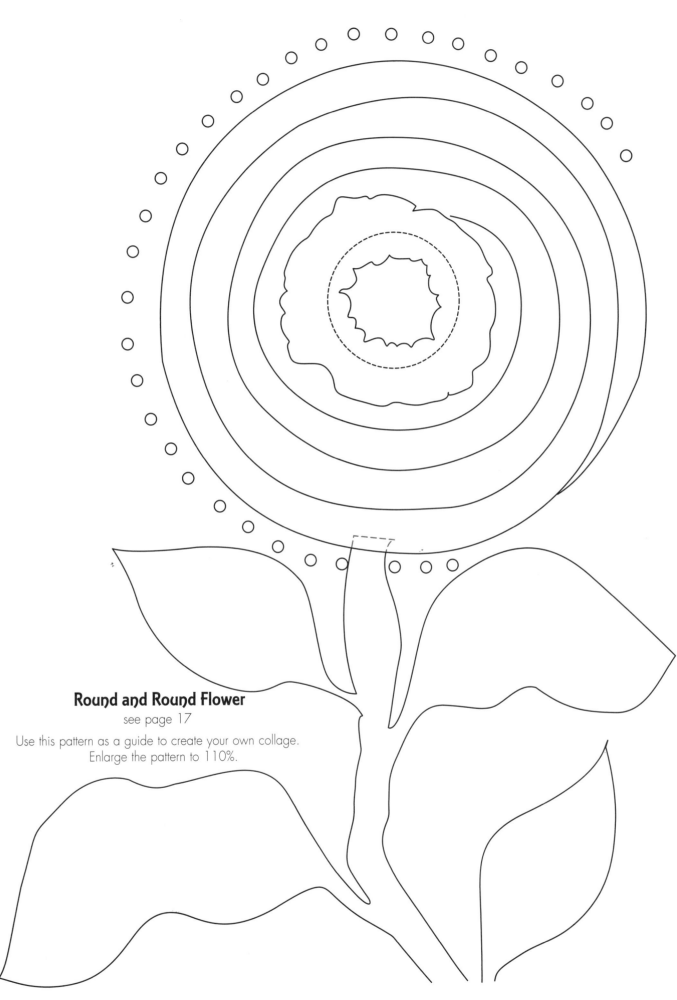

Round and Round Flower

see page 17

Use this pattern as a guide to create your own collage.
Enlarge the pattern to 110%.

Tropical Flower

see page 24

Use this pattern as a guide to create your own collage.

Carry-All Purse

see pages 20 - 21

Use this pattern as a guide to create your own collage.

Face

**Elegant Lady
with Birds**
see page 29

Use this pattern as a guide to
create your own collage.
Enlarge the pattern to 120%.

Wing

bird

Neck

Leaves

Small Flower

Day in a Garden Shirt
see page 14
Use this pattern as a guide to
create your own collage.

Large Flower

Medium Flower

Postcards

see page 19

Use these patterns as a guide
to create your own collage.

Suppliers

Most craft and variety stores
carry an excellent assortment of
supplies. If you need something
special, ask your local store to
contact the following companies.

Markers & Alcohol Inks

SHARPIE MARKERS - CHISEL TIP
sanfordcorp.com

COPIC MARKERS and REFILL INKS
copicmarker.com

ALCOHOL INKS
rangerink.com

Fabrics & Threads

TAFFETA SILK
DellaQ.com

SILK SCARVES and SILK VELVET
dharmatradingco.com

DOUPIONI SILK
supersilk.com

PHOTO TRANSFER FABRIC
jacquardproducts.com

PEARL COTTON FLOSS
dmc-usa.com

Accessories

BENDABLE MUSLIN DOLLS
fibrecraft.com

FABRI-TAC ADHESIVE
beaconcreates.com

PIPETTE DROPPERS
d-originals.com

STAZON AND VERSACRAFT INK PADS
tsukineko.com

STAMPS and STENCILS
plaidonline.com
craftsetcwholesale.com
stampafe.com

MIST IT! MISTER
inspiredcafts.com

STEAM-A-SEAM 2
warmcompany.com

BEADED FRINGE
expointl.com

Tips on Silks and Fabrics

Collect a variety of White and light colored lace and fabrics in different weights
(lightweight canvas, bleached muslin, China Silk, Taffeta Silk), fabric textures (woven, knit,
organza) and fibers (Silk, Cotton and Synthetic). Permanent markers and Alcohol Ink colors are
equally beautiful on almost any fiber and fabric.

Test Dye Patterns with Inexpensive Coffee Filters - Use white coffee filters with a fluted or pleated
edge. Mist filters with water then iron them flat. Test color patterns with markers, inks and alcohol.
These work similar to fabric and are inexpensive. Save the dyed filters for reference.

Washability - The Permanent Markers and Alcohol Inks used in this book were designed for paper.
They work amazingly well on fabrics. The colors are best suited to small Stitched Collages and
Art Quilts that don't require washing. The colors fade a little with each washing. I rinse my
fabrics in cold water after dyeing and heat setting to be sure any excess residue is removed.

Tips for Working with Fabrics - Most cottons, synthetics, satins, laces, ribbons and threads dye
very well. I used regular cotton bleached muslin or wrinkle free muslin for many dyed items.
Cotton fabrics usually have a matte finish. I love dyeing silks because the colors have a
wonderful brilliance and sheen. All the fabrics I tested dyed well without prewashing.

China Silk fabric and scarves (lightweight Habotai silk) dye really well. Because it is thin,
the colors run and bleed to produce amazing patterns. China Silk absorbs a minimal amount of
color, and it dries faster than other fabrics. When sewing this fabric, I suggest that you back it
with fusible lightweight interfacing to keep it from being slippery in your sewing machine.

Taffeta Silk is wonderful and accepts Permanent Marker and Alcohol Ink dyes very well. If
you do wash this fabric, the edges will ravel creating a wonderful narrow fringe effect that
looks great in Stitched Collage pieces. This fabric has a nice woven body and sews well.

Dupioni Silk accepts the colors and really has a beautiful sheen. Some Dupioni silks have
more of a nubby texture than others (I like the nubby ones best). This fabric sews well.

Silk Velvet, Satin and Cutwork dye rich and beautiful. They make fabulous scarves.